"Harriet Hope Green has given us the best of her expertise in working with children and her creative talents for helping those who struggle with challenges. Through delightfully fresh activities and ideas, Harriet Hope Green provides the reader with a step-by-step instructional 'how to' that will be appreciated by educators and parents alike!"

—*Wilma Fellman, M.Ed., Licensed Professional Counselor and author of* The Other Me: Poetic Thoughts on ADD for Adults, Kids and Parents, *Michigan*

"Harriet Hope Green has tutored my daughter for several years, and has introduced many of the creative ideas in the book. I marvel at how much the activities in this book can alter the mood of an often dreaded homework session. The creative activities help students forget they are doing homework. My daughter looks forward to 'Miss Harriet's' tutoring visits because they are fun and effective."

—*Kim Roehl, parent of a child with multiple learning challenges, Michigan*

"I think giant steps helped me learn my basic multiplication facts. The mystery box was so much fun. All the activities helped me be successful."

—*G., student aged 12, diagnosed with AD/HD and dyslexia, Michigan*

"Homework is often a source of stress for students with AD/HD, their parents, and teachers. This book provides lots of tips, strategies, and activities that encourage fun and creativity in finding new solutions; such as doing homework under the table! A useful new toolkit for facing the brick wall of homework."

—*Joanne Steer, Chartered Clinical Psychologist and co-author of* Helping Kids and Teens with ADHD in School, *UK*

AD/HD
HOMEWORK
CHALLENGES
TRANSFORMED!

of related interest

Organize Your ADD/ADHD Child
A Practical Guide for Parents
Cheryl R. Carter
ISBN 978 1 84905 839 1

Step by Step Help for Children with ADHD
A Self-Help Manual for Parents
Cathy Laver-Bradbury, Margaret Thompson, Anne Weeks, David Daley and Edmund J. S. Sonuga-Barke
ISBN 978 1 84905 070 8

ADHD – Living without Brakes
Martin L. Kutscher MD
Illustrated by Douglas Puder, M.D.
ISBN 978 1 84310 873 3 Hardback
ISBN 978 1 84905 816 2 Paperback

Helping Kids and Teens with ADHD in School
A Workbook for Classroom Support and Managing Transitions
Joanne Steer and Kate Horstmann
Illustrated by Jason Edwards
ISBN 978 1 84310 663 0

Count Me In!
Ideas for Actively Engaging Students in Inclusive Classrooms
Richard Rose and Michael Shevlin
Foreword by Paul Cooper
Part of the Innovative Learning for All series

HARRIET HOPE GREEN

AD/HD HOMEWORK CHALLENGES TRANSFORMED!

CREATIVE WAYS TO ACHIEVE FOCUS AND ATTENTION BY BUILDING ON AD/HD TRAITS

Jessica Kingsley *Publishers*
London and Philadelphia

Front cover image source: iStockphoto ®. The cover image is for
illustrative purposes only, and any person featuring is a model.

First published in 2012
by Jessica Kingsley Publishers
116 Pentonville Road
London N1 9JB, UK
and
400 Market Street, Suite 400
Philadelphia, PA 19106, USA

www.jkp.com

Library of Congress Cataloging in Publication Data
Green, Harriet Hope.
  AD/HD homework challenges transformed! : creative ways to achieve focus and
attention by building on ad/hd traits / Harriet Hope Green.
    p. cm.
  Includes index.
  ISBN 978-1-84905-880-3 (alk. paper)
  1. Attention-deficit-disordered children--Education. 2. Attention-deficit
hyperactivity disorder. 3. Homework. 4. Home and school. I. Title.
  LC4713.2.G74 2012
  371.94--dc23
                                    2011033473

British Library Cataloguing in Publication Data
A CIP catalogue record for this book is available from the British Library

ISBN 978 1 84905 880 3
eISBN 978 0 85700 601 1

Printed and bound in Great Britain

This book is dedicated to all the children who created such wonderful illustrations for it.

Contents

Preface

Homework time with AD/HD students can be a nightmare for both parents and students. *AD/HD Homework Challenges Transformed!* is a book filled with creative methods to motivate the AD/HD child during homework time. The activities in the book empower, engage, enable, enrich, and encourage children. Student needs are addressed and the child is motivated to reach a goal. The ideas are geared to AD/HD students in grades K–8 (ages 5–13), and also would be effective with *all* elementary school students (ages 5–10).

Current literature and activity books aimed at working with AD/HD students appear to focus on restricting, sterilizing the environment (no distractions), managing break times, dividing work tasks, rewarding, and adjusting medication. Some of these techniques are incorporated in this book by using child-centered activities that empower students, but this book is unique because the characteristics and symptoms of AH/HD are mobilized and activated as vehicles to do the homework. Success and a positive experience are the goals for parents and students.

Introduction

Most AD/HD students arrive home from school exhausted after a day of criticism from teachers and teasing from peers. At times, the student is frustrated and confused, and cannot understand what went on during the day. That day may have been spent staring out the window, acting out, tapping a pencil, looking for supplies, and probably visiting the bathroom and drinking fountain excessively.

Work with the AD/HD population makes it abundantly clear that a unique approach is required to conquer the homework challenge. Homework activities that *empower, engage, enrich, enable,* and *encourage,* combined with educationally justified "fun," can alter the homework atmosphere. Students are encouraged to take an active part in the homework process and to enjoy the success.

Strategies suggested in this book should be selected with the student's individual needs in mind. Use those games that are effective with your child. Have fun with the homework.

Empowering allows a child to feel some control in the quest to complete homework. The parent empowers the child by offering choices, all of which relate to homework completion. This is "guided empowerment."

For example, you might offer a choice between starting with math homework and starting with science homework, or the student might select a place to work: bedroom or dining-room table. The student makes the decision and feels somewhat in control. Although not all educators agree, many believe that use of calculators and spellers can be empowering for the AD/HD student. Using this equipment allows the student to think about processes instead of facts and words, which are easily gathered with tools.

A student is *engaged* when actively involved in the task. He is part of the process. For example, you might switch roles with the child. Allow him to quiz you after a reading a short excerpt from the homework assignment. Allow him to find your mistakes in a math problem. Another way to keep the student engaged is by acknowledging the need to move. Encourage him to "jump" answers to math facts, or walk up one step every time a correct answer is given. He could explain the directions to an activity so you can understand. Many activities in *AD/HD Homework Challenges Transformed!* promote traits of the disorder as a means to completing homework.

Enrich constantly. Share your experiences. Tell a personal story about how you did a science experiment, tell a joke, share a trick that will make assignments easier, show a silly picture that demonstrates the concept, and even ask the student to make up a game for the homework. The silly stories will enhance recall. Break words up into fun parts to enhance spelling. Explain what happened when you forgot your math facts. Did your dog eat your social studies paper? Read together in a new environment such as the sofa or back porch.

When you *enable*, you allow the student to feel success. In this book, tasks are presented to give the student a positive experience. For example, you might encourage a reluctant reader to start with a book two grades below level. That almost guarantees comprehension. This "easy" book can help the student learn strategies that make reading a fun experience. Allow her to formulate alternate endings and make them weird or fun. She can "be the teacher" and ask you questions after each page. When doing math, start from the "known" and build on that. Show the math tricks you learned. Teaching for success is the key to this skill.

Encouragement is mandatory. Notice and compliment every bit of success. Look for the positive. Children love to hear the "good stuff" when you notice their positive physical and academic attributes. Notice clothing, eye color, how a pencil is held, handwriting, or neat backpack. And, even more importantly, notice progress in school work, great focusing, good thinking, or great comprehension. You cannot bestow enough positives. Some strategies in this book include short games that create success experiences. The games are academically oriented and created for success.

Not all strategy games presented are suitable for every student. The type of activity and when you use it will be dependent upon the student's needs. Some strategies use physical movement, some enable focus, and some enrich academics. All are directed toward the needs of the AD/HD or reluctant learner and completing homework without tears.

Before starting homework, make certain that the child knows that there will be breaks during the homework time. If work looks overwhelming to the student, progress is difficult because his focus is on the task ahead. The thought of sitting still that long can impede progress. Make it clear that the breaks will be timed (usually 15–20 minutes) and restarting after a break is imperative. Parents need to be alert to the child's need for a rest. If the wiggles and an inability to focus are apparent, of course a break is in order. If, however, the student is totally absorbed in a task, sometimes the break can wait.

The local dollar store will become your very best friend. A stroll through the store reveals a myriad of items that can be helpful with homework and many organizational and high-interest activities with the AD/HD student. There are hundreds of ways to color code, and many things students can sort when concentration wanes. There are fancy folders, wonderful stickers, containers, planners, calendars, squishy balls, pipe cleaners. The walk through will help you generate some ideas for activities not mentioned in this book. Sensory activities are particularly appealing to someone who needs to "do" something.

If medication is part of the child's daily routine, it should be on the morning "To Do" chart, and it is important to be consistent. The pill could be waiting next to a glass of milk or orange juice. You might wish to monitor the swallow. Children who are drug-resistant develop all sorts of methods to sabotage the procedure. The pill can stay under the tongue, be placed in a pocket, or fed to a nearby plant.

Whether to use medication on weekends and vacations is a difficult decision. Two schools of thought exist. One compares the pill to wearing glasses. Is there a need to wear glasses on weekends and vacations? The pill is an aid just like glasses. On the other hand, some parents want to give the child a vacation from medication, especially if the medication causes personality alteration. Sometimes a child will request the medication. This is a difficult decision for parents. Once the decision is made, it is important to be consistent.

I recommend that a parent should always carry an AD/HD survival kit when the child will be in the public eye. If the child with AD/HD has a meltdown in public, the kit can be used to temper the meltdown. The kit needs to be portable, should contain small items such as a notebook, crayons, a squish ball, straws, pipe cleaners, hand-held game, and Silly Putty. All busy activities qualify.

Rewards and consequences for the AD/HD student present another difficult decision for the parent. Short-term, work-related consequences are recommended. Minimal infringements should have minimal consequences. Forbidding a favorite video game for a week as a consequence does not relate to forgetting an assignment. Instead, maybe a new procedure could be instituted. For example, from now on, the book bag is emptied, sorted, and compared to the planner every day *before* snack time. If needed, a return to school for a paper or book may be necessary. *Do not* deny the snack. Rewards (a poker chip, a marble, a card, a sticker, etc.) should be distributed immediately after the task is complete. These symbols then can be traded in for non-material rewards such as lunch in a restaurant with Mom, a game that Mom can play with the student, the opportunity to select the menu for dinner for two nights, or an extra hour of reading before bedtime.

One-on-one time is a very special reward. There is a chapter in the book entitled "Emotions." The activities in this chapter are not directly related to homework, but do reinforce academic skills. The activities serve as vehicles for self-expression. AD/HD students need a way to express themselves. These students are subjected to a number of negative experiences and often keep strong emotions locked up inside. They are not always willing to discuss these frustrations with their parents. The activities in this chapter offer an opportunity for expression even though the student does not realize this. When children participate in the creative dramatics and activate imaginations, a lot of emotion might be expressed.

All activities in this book are dependent on parental support. When the parent can be there to positively reinforce, demonstrate, and generate, the student can be encouraged and enriched. The parent serves as a cheerleader and is there to instill confidence. Once the student has integrated the skills and is empowered, the parent can allow the student to work independently. The AD/HD student needs all the encouragement possible. The parent supplies that with love, hugs, verbal comments, tokens for rewards, and incentives to succeed. In turn, the parent could benefit from two aspirin, a dose of patience, and a lot of encouraging words.

A parent must grasp any opportunity to address the symptoms of AD/HD. This means providing opportunities for success experiences whenever possible. After-school sports are highly recommended. The sport might offer a success experience and can provide other positives. The child would be part of a team and social skills could be practiced. The AD/HD child is a bundle of zest and energy. This is an opportunity to work off that energy. If possible, the games should be right after school so homework time can start when some of the energy has been spent.

In this book the word "child" is used to describe children of both genders and the use of "he" and "she" is alternated. This is done for ease of reading only, and is not intended to reflect any gender bias.

1
Enablers

The activities in this chapter are homework openers that address the session in an enjoyable way. They help to establish a positive attitude. The first activity, *Scavenger Hunt*, engages the student, involves movement, and clarifies the task, allowing the student to feel successful from the beginning. There are a variety of opening activities, so the parent can vary the experience. The activities in this chapter address all the themes in this book: they encourage, enable, enrich, engage, and empower.

Scavenger Hunt

Make a list of all the supplies the child needs to complete the day's homework. Include paper, pencil, book, scissors, ruler, planner, backpack, and anything else necessary for the task so the student does not need to leave his seat during the session. The student then goes on a *timed* scavenger hunt through the house to locate everything on the list. Each item should be checked off when located. This activity engages the child in the organization process, encourages focus, and helps get the homework process started in an enjoyable manner. Below is a sample list. Everyone's needs will be different. Perhaps the hunt could be completed faster the next day.

This activity is engaging and empowering.

Scavenger hunt suggestions

☐ Book   ☐ Erasers

☐ Book   ☐ Crayons

☐ Book   ☐ Scissors

☐ Glue   ☐ Small notebook

☐ Ruler   ☐ Planner

☐ Backpack   ☐ Protractor

☐ Compass   ☐ Tape

☐ Sharp pencils   ☐ Computer

☐ Highlighter   ☐ Lamp

☐ Calculator

Sock it to Me

This activity is an interesting way to start the homework session. Begin by placing an easily identifiable object (marble, spoon, etc.) in a sock and ask the child to identify the object without looking. Once this is done, ask the child to fill the sock with another item so you can try to identify it tomorrow. This takes a second and is great for empowering and enriching the child. Also, it becomes something to remember, which is often difficult for the AD/HD student. Ignore the game if the student forgets the sock the next day. Do not ask for the sock; it will show up eventually.

This is a game of responsibility and almost guaranteed success.

Balance Ball

When a student sits on a balance (exercise) ball, much-needed movement is enabled. Of course, when the ball is introduced, there will be extensive experimentation, investigation, and exploration. After the initial investigation, the ball becomes the student's chair, and the student can take part in productive work time while sitting on the ball. The movement accommodates the student's need to expend energy while completing homework. These large ball-chairs are great for posture and balance, enrich the homework situation, and help the student to engage. The parent might enjoy sitting on a ball, too.

These balls enrich and enable the child.

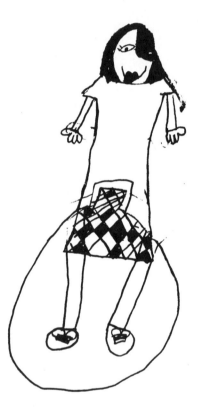

The Folder to Remember

Plastic accordion-type folders (available where you buy school supplies) have six to eight separate pockets. This type of folder can be very helpful to the AD/HD student as an organizational system and a way to help remember homework. The tabs can be used as subject dividers, and the child can help decide which tab goes with which subject. The decision engages the student, who can also be empowered by decorating the folder using crayons or stickers. This gives a sense of ownership. There should be one unlabeled pocket at the front of the folder. The front section should be designated for homework. All papers that move back and forth between school and home are placed in this section. The folder will be a novelty for the student at first. It will help some students with organization, but others may be overwhelmed with the process. If it is too difficult, the student should have only one folder labeled "*Homework.*" This folder is useful with *It's in the Box* (page 39) and *Mail Person on the Run* (page 57).

This activity empowers and encourages the student.

Planner Art

There are several ways to enable students to use a color-coding system to help organizational skills. The accordion folder is a great place to start color coding. Sticky notes, sticky tabs, tongue depressors, miniature clips, paper clips, and any other colorful things from the dollar store can be used. The colors can be manipulated any way the student selects. One color for each subject can be established and used for everything in one class. Encourage the student to select the colors and carry it through from planner to folder to homework. For example, red sticky notes can be used for math. The note can be placed in the planner as a homework reminder. Then red can go in the text, and on any math reminders. Some students find this confusing, however; if it can't be used in school, the color system can be used at home to label drawers or keep track of tasks. The dollar store is a treasure chest of organizational ideas.

This activity engages and enables

Reliable Best Buddy

AD/HD students have difficulty with the paper trail. Papers do not get home, papers are not complete, papers are complete but not handed in, the homework planner is blank or incomplete, and often supplies in the backpack are not coordinated with the assignment expected. Every AD/HD student needs a homework buddy. Ideally, the buddy should be a responsible "teacher pleaser." Parents should discuss the plan with the buddy's parents early in the school year. The need to contact a buddy for direction should be treated as a great idea rather than an embarrassment or punishment. Calling a buddy for an assignment enables the child and helps avoid negativity in school the next day.

This activity empowers and enables.

Recording Pen

Many AD/HD behaviors can be addressed with a pen that includes a very small digital sound recorder. Students use the pen to take notes while the lecture is being recorded. The recording can be used during homework time to assist both parent and student.

The recorder can be used for several purposes. It can record homework assignments as the teacher assigns them. It can be used to record lectures and assignments, and to compensate for a student's difficulty with focus. This device is probably more appropriate for older students. It can be purchased in most electronics stores.

This pen offers the opportunity for the child to be empowered, enabled, engaged, encouraged, and enriched.

Success for All to See

The AD/HD student cannot get enough praise. The child needs to feel special whenever possible. Opportunities to excel in sports, art, music, computer skills, and anywhere else should be provided. Because of impulsivity and lack of social skills, the AD/HD student encounters negativity from many people in the environment—teachers, peers, parents, and siblings. The parent should take advantage of any opportunity to emphasize the positive in the child. A great way to do this is to display large, colorful symbols of her successes. The display should be visible to her first thing in the morning and last thing before sleep. Trace over the outline of a star on the next page to create many colorful stars. Whenever she does something positive, the feat should be noted on a star. Then the stars can be hung in her room or used to make a border. The positives need not all be academic. They might include getting to breakfast on time, a good mark in school, a goal in hockey, or remembering to say "please" and "thank you." Before lights out, review all the things written on the stars. Use any excuse to write on a star.

This is an enabling idea.

Stepping Forward

This activity is a visual representation of success. It will be obvious to all who enter the home. Trace the child's foot and use the outline to cut many more feet. Each time the student is successful, write the success experience on a paper foot. The foot is placed on the floor leading to the child's bedroom. The starting point can be determined by parent and child together. When the steps reach the student's bedroom, some non-material reward might be offered.

This activity encourages and rewards.

Parent as Secretary

Expressive writing not only requires a complex thought process, but also could mean handwriting. Sometimes this can take a long time, and the student sees only a long task ahead. With so much to think about, panic can set in and an "I can't" attitude prevails. A parent can address the problem by becoming the student's secretary. When the parent is a secretary, the handwriting problem disappears. The parent can pose questions to help get the thoughts on paper without adding information. When complete, the parent should ask the child to read the paper. If possible, the student should use the computer to write the paper. If not, perhaps arrangements can be made with the teacher to accept the adult's handwriting. The child's thinking process is the important part, not the handwriting.

This enables the student to have a successful experience with writing. It empowers the child because there is a neat product to give to the teacher.

Give Me the Signal

There are signs all around. Some of them are informational, some are directional, and some can symbolize danger. There are some signs that have only a picture and, although AD/HD students are usually familiar with restroom signs and stop signs, the ability to interpret some pictures might be very difficult for one who struggles with working memory.

It is important that the student becomes familiar with common signs and that he understands that some signs have pictures that represent a message. To reinforce this idea, ask the student to make some signs (no words) that could represent things in the home. He might illustrate toothpaste being squeezed at the bottom, do not enter, reading zone, and any other ideas that require communication. Have him explain the signs.

This activity is both enabling and empowering.

The Schedule

The AD/HD student has difficulty with the concept of time which leads to difficulties with scheduling. Time and scheduling can be addressed in this activity. Look at the various charts and grids available online, many of which are free. Allow the student to select the perfect chart after being given directions. First, ask her to create the daily schedule in school. If it is realistic, encourage the addition of times. Then she selects another chart to present the weekly schedule. Depending upon the student's abilities, a monthly schedule could also be created. A yearly schedule of holidays could be created. This is not a "one time only" activity. Schedules can be addressed on "no homework days," or just for fun. Illustrations might be a part of the schedules.

This activity enables, enriches, and encourages.

Mix and Match

This activity addresses both concentration and the wiggles. It is a sorting exercise that easily could be a part of your travel survival kit. I recommend using packages of tiny multicolored pompom balls. They are soft, lightweight, and easily transportable. The child must separate the balls into same-color groups. Some movement, some thinking, immediate success, and distraction are addressed in this activity. You can use any supplies that can be sorted by shape, color, or composition.

This simple game serves well in doctors' offices, restaurants, and at the dinner table. It engages, encourages, and enables.

Mystery Box

A mystery box provides a high-interest, calming activity that children like to do over and over again. Additionally, it is a mobile game that guarantees success. It helps pass time when children must wait, and is a favorite reward.

The parent should create a curious-looking box with interesting decorations. The box is named Mystery Box. Fill the box with all sorts of household items. Use a spoon, toothbrush, toothpick, key, lipstick tube, dog bone, sponge, pencil, marker, etc. You can add things all the time.

The game is played with the child standing in front of you, with his back to you, with eyes closed and hands held behind the back. The parent places a "mystery" item from the box in the hands and the child must identify the object using tactile clues only. You may want to expand the game using smell and other sensory experiences. Mystery Box should be used sparingly as children can tire of it.

This activity encourages and enriches.

The Timer Says it All

Time is an important factor while the AD/HD student does homework. It is vital that he knows there will be breaks. He may believe there is an insurmountable amount of homework and can envision working all night.

Breaks are important for two reasons. First, the AD/HD student must have the opportunity to move around. Second, breaks provide time for the child to relax in order to garner energy to focus after the break. Time should be regulated based on the student's age and performance level. If assigned workloads from school are unrealistically time consuming, parent and teacher might discuss accommodations for the child. A silent clock in the work area should be visible only to the parent. Breaks should be dictated by observing the child. The parent will know when a change is necessary, judging by his behavior. Breaks should never exceed 15–20 minutes, and the child needs to understand how important it is to start working again immediately after the break.

The clock should not be visible to the student until break time. Then display the clock, so the student can show you where the hands will be when break time is over.

Time is an important consideration for AD/HD students in many other ways. Time consistency is vital. Mealtimes, bedtimes, alarm times, and pill times (if applicable) should be the same day to day. Time limits give a sense of security. The timer can engage and empower the child.

Yes, I Can

This activity enables the student to exercise some control of the learning session while the parent sets the parameters. A parent can offer the child two alternatives (both leading to homework completion). For example, the parent might allow the child to decide to do math or science next. Or the parent might empower the student to read the book silently or read aloud. Another choice might be between doing the assignment on a computer or by hand. The field of choice is narrowed, and the child is empowered and will engage in reaching the goal.

This is an enriching activity.

Geographical Location

It is important for a child to be able to describe a location. At first, she can describe location using her body as a reference point. Words such as right, left, up, down, in, next, under, and over will be used. Slowly introduce standard geographical terms. To refine these skills, allow the child to make a simple map of the home. Ask for a description of various locations on the map. Next she can use neighborhood maps to describe location. Home, library, and school should be placed on the map. Map symbols and compass directions can be included. It is important for the child to understand map symbols. Give her a land map (there are many on the internet). Use this map to help her set up a map key using symbols. Depending upon student age and ability, some things to include on the key are North and South Poles, Equator, boundaries, longitude, latitude, mile/kilometer, continents, oceans, lakes, and mountains. Most of these concepts will be presented in school. Review is important. Start with familiar places and work into more complex maps. When working on "real" maps, "find me" games requiring use of geographical terms can be played.

These activities are enriching and empowering.

2 Study Skills

The activities in this chapter allow the child to participate in some interesting activities which reinforce the study skills required for academic success. Processing question/answer requirements, learning the importance of rules by playing a game, and following directions are explored. These skills are appropriate for any academic requirements. The activities also reinforce sequencing and decision making. They can be used on an as-needed basis, or can be used as separate learning experiences. These activities have implications for the AD/HD child's future.

It's in the Box

Students of all ages benefit from this activity. It can become something of a game. The student brings the backpack and binder to the place of study. Usually dog-eared papers are falling out from all sides, and everything is poorly organized. Bring a box to the table, and ask the student to look at the papers one at a time to make some decisions. He separates the papers into three piles: a pile to keep in the backpack and binder, a pile to trash, and a pile to keep in the box. The pile to keep in the box includes all papers that need to be kept, but don't need to be carried around daily. The student makes the decisions and does not have to part with papers that are treasured.

This activity empowers the student, helps organize papers and resources, and controls distractions.

The Project

The long-term project is almost inevitable. It is vital that the parent knows about the project the minute it is assigned. There could be a plan with the teacher to keep parents informed of big projects. The child must be actively engaged at all stages and empowered to make decisions. Even though the parent may not agree with the decisions, it is the student's project. Usually, the teacher will make an outline plan, and directions will be clear. Grade level is determined by the extent and quality of the project. I would encourage the parent to sit with the child for a planning session, so the parent can help set reasonable goals. The project must be broken down into workable parts, and a realistic timeline should be established. Below are some suggestions for working on a long-term project with an AD/HD student.

The parent can help enrich the experience by inviting the student to help shopping for supplies. Projects tend to overwhelm many students. Work on them can empower and enrich.

Project pointers

Use the suggestions that are suitable for the student's age, abilities, grade level, and the project requirement.

1. Have a pocket calendar ready. The student needs to see the time span between this day and due day. Then work time can be planned. The parent should assist the child in breaking down the work required for the project. Keep the segments small if possible. This is empowering as students often have difficulty relating time to goals. The student is engaged putting goals on the calendar. The goals must include allowing time to complete the required research or reading while allowing sufficient days for completing artwork, presentation, or demonstration. It is important to stress the time/goal relationship while helping to divide the work into reasonable segments.

2. If artwork is required, the child should make a list of all materials needed. This is often difficult for the AD/HD student. Making a list requires focus, future planning, and organization. The parent should allow the child to make the list before making any suggestions. A special trip to the store to purchase required materials is a reward because it creates an opportunity for special time with a parent. It also helps the child to act on plans.

3. Any technology required is usually familiar to the student. When working with the technology, the child may need limits in terms of time, quality, and quantity. It might be a good idea to monitor the activity. The use of technology is engaging and empowering, but it also can be very distracting.

4. Note cards and their organization will depend on the assignment. To help the AD/HD student with note cards, the most important thing to do is create visible divisions. Use colored note cards so that the student can see the different parts of the project. For example, for a project about a country or city, red cards might be used for history, while green cards might represent information on climate. Each color (part) should be kept separate, so encourage the use of multiple columns, each one headed by a large visual title. The divisions must be clearly delineated. This process enables a student to envision small parts rather than becoming overwhelmed by a mass of information.

5. Paraphrasing and plagiarizing should be explained. Use the following game to encourage paraphrasing. Ask the child to read a paragraph from a research source. As soon as the paragraph is complete, cover the paragraph and ask the child to tell you about two things that were read. It might be helpful to use the "who, what, where, when, and how" approach.

6. The type of notes, sentences, or words used will vary with age, ability, and project requirements.

7. Adhering to the schedule is vital. It provides the structure an AD/HD student needs. The project may not fit into regular homework time, so there may need to be additional built-in project time.

8. Encourage the student to refer continually to the project directions/plan so that requirements are totally understood.

Question over Answer

Note taking and studying for exams are challenges for AD/HD students. Sometimes, notes are non-existent, and if there are any notes, organization is often lacking. To help to consolidate information and associate it with potential questions, a stenographer's notebook is recommended. Each page should be folded in half by bringing the bottom of the page up to the spiral. A question can be written on the part of the page facing out, and the answer can be written under the fold. Parents might help the student, and each significant word or concept could be placed on a separate page of the notebook.

If the student is enabled, the process of setting up the notebook is a great study method. This activity enables students while encouraging study. You might take turns asking and answering questions using the notebook. When all information is in one place, the student is empowered to succeed. Tokens might be awarded for each correct response.

Scientific Method

A simple science experiment at home can help the child with AD/HD to practice sequencing, follow through, and directions, and with responsibility, while learning the scientific method. The internet is filled with age-appropriate science experiments. Most are quite simple. The parent should monitor, but not help the student. Allow the student to select an experiment, do it, and, if necessary, make observations. An experiment that requires daily observations is great. While doing the experiment, the scientific method (materials, hypotheses, procedure, results, and conclusion) should be stressed. Each part should be completed by the student.

The experiment itself requires the use of many basic skills, but also enriches, engages, and encourages.

Karaoke

Place a microphone in a student's hand, and there is a good chance you will hear results. This is a wonderful activity to use in math when basic facts are required. Ask the child to sing the facts to a child-created tune or use a tune the child selects. When multiplying, for example, the student can sing "8, 16, 24, 32, 40, 48, 56, 64, 72, and 80." You can use this method with the doubles and squares in addition and multiplication. Perhaps it would be fun to sing spelling words.

This activity is enabling, encouraging, and empowering, and might even be fun.

Crystal Ball

Thinking about the future, both immediate and far off, can be difficult for the impulsive AD/HD student who cannot always contemplate consequences. Using a crystal ball is an excellent way to help the child focus on the future. Allow the student to hold something that represents a crystal ball, and ask that the future be told about someone in the family. All predictions must be happy, fun, and upbeat. The predicted futures can be written down by parent or student. The student can decide who to use as a subject. It might be interesting to hear the child's self-predictions.

This activity is enriching and engaging, and empowers the student.

Memories

Few people escape the memory monster during their school years. If you are not memorizing spelling words, you are memorizing states and countries, math facts, or the Periodic Table. Memorizing is particularly difficult for the student who cannot sit still or focus. There is no single magic memory technique to teach students, but there are many methods to try. Since movement assists the AD/HD student, you can use a staircase and designate each step as a spelling word, math fact, or answer to a question. Each correct answer represents a step upward. A mistake means a step down. You can determine a destination and the child can jump to it. Jumping words is fun. Some spelling programs use shape around the words as a learning technique. By outlining the shape of a word, tall letters and letters that fall below the line become obvious. This method gives a visual clue to the student. Sometimes it can be helpful if you associate the answer with a silly story. Singing the multiplication tables can also be fun. A student can walk the eights and jump the threes. It is important that the student "sees" the progress. Flash cards are great because they allow the child to see the problem. Using multiple methods is desirable.

This skill engages the student, and the parent provides the encouragement. Memory empowers the child and can be enabling.

Put it Together

Using a Venn diagram (like the one shown below) is an organizational study technique that is very useful to the AD/HD student. It is particularly helpful because it is a visual representation that does not often include many words at first. It is fun to fill out the diagram. When comparing two things, the part marked A would have the characteristics of one item. The part marked C would have the characteristics of the second item. The part marked B would include a list of characteristics both items have in common. For example, if I compare a carrot (Part A) to a tomato (Part C), the characteristics of the carrot are in Part A. Part A includes these words: orange, chewy, and hard to bite. Part C, the tomato, would include: red, soft, mushy, has seeds. Part B would show the following similarities: vegetable, healthy, in salads, and food.

This activity empowers and enables.

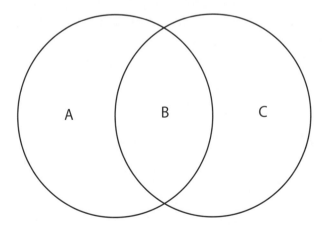

Clever Solutions

Math is a subject that addresses the challenges of focus, organization, and executive function. The student can express solutions in a number of ways that embrace AD/HD behaviors. The answer to 5 – 3 can be jumped. It can be answered with giant steps. The answer to the problem 6 + 7 can be clapped. An answer can be expressed with jumping jacks or toe touches. Large side-steps and backward steps are other ways to express answers.

The student is engaged, enabled, and enriched.

Create a Question

This activity can be used in all subjects. Write answers on index cards, and challenge the student to create the question for each card. This method can be used for math facts, vocabulary, or questions in science and social studies. It might be interesting to award one token for each correct answer. The tokens could be redeemed immediately to add minutes to break time.

This activity is empowering and engaging

3 Bring on the Homework

This chapter addresses a variety of academic skills. The activities enable students to practice some basic skills that will affect homework assignments now and in the future. The student is asked to teach, find signal words in written material, and follow directions. Students explore various work venues in order to find the environment that suits them best. The skills are building blocks that can help the student face future assignments with some confidence. Self-concept soars when children can use pre-learned skills in new assignments.

Pick the Stick

A jar full of colored tongue depressors can be used in many ways when working with an AD/HD student. It empowers the student by offering choices for homework completion. Some alternatives suggested will require teacher approval. For example, tongue depressors can be used to determine how to do math homework. A suggestion is written on each depressor. In math, suggestions could be: do work on another sheet of paper, show your work right under the problem, read all problems out loud, circle the answer to each problem, check paper to make certain you did all assigned work. In reading, choices could include: read the page aloud, read the page silently, write two questions about the page, find two words that are new to you, tell me about your favorite character. Sometimes students like to pick a stick to use during break time. Suggestions on the sticks might be: jog around the block, 20 minutes of computer time, 20 minutes of favorite technology, call a friend, play a game.

This activity is empowering, engaging, and enriching.

The Unexpected Reward

This technique should be used infrequently so that it retains its value to the student. The parent can place a card that describes a reward in a box. Boxes can be wrapped with bright wrapping paper and ribbon. The boxes contain one reward such as a token, coupon or note for special privileges or later bedtimes. After a particularly wonderful homework session, boxes can appear. The child selects one box, opens it, and the parent explains reasons for the reward. Do not reward every good session, but often enough that the child will strive for productive homework time. The boxes can be brought out whenever there are significant accomplishments.

This activity encourages and enriches.

Student as Teacher

Sequencing and dealing with multi-step activities are challenges for the AD/HD student. Creating situations that allow students to practice these skills is helpful. Ask the child to teach *you* how to do something that requires sequencing. It is important to stress that some things must be done in order. You can be taught how to retrieve email, play a computer game, do a math problem, scramble an egg, or make a bed. This enables the child to deal with a number of steps that require sequencing. Skills are enriched, and learner becomes teacher.

This activity is empowering and encouraging.

Topic Sentence to Concluding Sentence

Written expression requires organization. Organizational skills are challenging for the AD/HD child. Thoughts are rushing, and concentration on one topic is not easy. In order to help the student with organization in written composition, it is helpful to concentrate on the first and last sentence of a paragraph. Introductions and conclusions should be taught by example. For example, demonstrate that a topic sentence could be "Everyone in this family is helpful." The concluding sentence could be "When everyone is helpful, many things get done." The child could fill in three middle sentences. Below are examples of opening and closing sentences. See if the student can identify these parts and explain her choice.

This activity will enable the student to begin working with the writing process and empower the student to use these skills.

Topic or concluding sentences

Ask the child to place a T or a C next to each sentence to indicate if it is a topic or concluding sentence. The child must be prepared to explain why. Some sentences might need both letters.

___ Recess time should be longer because...

___ So, a long recess time can have many advantages.

___ Breakfast is an important meal for many reasons.

___ I will tell you all about my best friend.

___ Playing on the team was a great experience.

___ I love long vacations because you can do so many things such as...

___ Let the games begin.

___ That is why I love this school.

___ Good teachers have five important characteristics.

___ Dinner is my favorite meal because there are so many choices.

—— In conclusion, I believe that the family unit is very important.

—— It is for those reasons that I love my new team.

—— Learning to be a team player is important for these reasons.

—— Finally, I would like you to remember how to eat wisely.

—— When I have homework to finish, I start with easy things first.

—— The internet helps me with many things such as...

—— My friend has a dog that is a pain.

—— They all lived happily ever after.

—— At the end of the day, everything was done.

Highlight the Signal

Highlighters can be useful tools when used properly. Most students tend to highlight far too much. The tool can be used in almost any subject. In math, operation signs can be highlighted. Key words in math word problems can be highlighted. In other subjects, try to encourage underlining one sentence in a paragraph (the main idea). In both math and English assignments, encourage the student to underline signal words—signal words help you remember what the question means. A newspaper or magazine could be used for main idea practice. Old math papers can be used to find signal words. Below is a list of common signal words for reading and language.

This activity enables and empowers.

Reading and language key words

- Change
- Compare
- Contrast
- Date
- Define
- Describe
- Explain
- Genre
- How
- How long
- Important
- In order
- Infer
- List
- Main idea
- Match
- Name
- Predict
- Replace
- Review
- Show
- Tell
- What
- When
- Where
- Which
- Who
- Why

Chart it, Reward it, Do it Again

AD/HD students are inundated with charts designed to encourage appropriate behavior and goal achievement. There are homework charts, schoolwork charts, progress charts, behavior charts, responsibility charts, chore charts, and reading progress charts. Charts are helpful for modifying behavior in some cases. However, charts tend to be minimally effective with the AD/HD student. Charts do not provide immediate gratification, and after a short amount of time the goals on the charts tend to bore AD/HD students. Charts usually include rules or commands. Instead of marking a chart daily, encourage the student to vocalize the rules, and offer a token for each correct response. When engaged in setting goals, the child buys into the program. This is enabling. Any chart should be limited to one week. Use of charts should be accompanied by a large amount of verbal praise.

This activity is engaging, enabling, and encouraging.

Follow Directions

This activity serves many purposes. It addresses some of the characteristics of AD/HD in game form while enabling, engaging, encouraging, enriching, and empowering the student. This game can be used when restlessness sets in, but when a full break is not warranted. First, tell the child to do three things: touch the table, run to the kitchen, and sit in the big chair. Things must be done in order. The first three are usually done easily. Give four directions the next time. Each time a direction is given, try to include one part that increases physical activity (five jumping jacks, run up the stairs, jump ten times, go from room to room, etc.).

The child has fun, uses memory, processes information, and is engaged, enriched, and enabled.

Where are You?

A change of venue can make the homework time a pleasure. You might wish to use this as a reward or simply for an interesting change. Allow the student to do homework in a sleeping bag. Alternatively, you can use bed sheets to drape over furniture to create a tent where homework can be completed. Doing homework under a table can be productive. The change in venue should be used on rare occasions so that it is a treat.

This activity enables and encourages.

4 Reading Dilemma

Reading involves many cognitive processes which means that for many AD/HD students it is a dreaded task. It involves focus, sequencing, critical thinking, and attention. These are the skills that are most difficult for the restless, impulsive, distracted, and forgetful student. This chapter includes some activities that might take the sting out of reading. By encouraging and enabling, a student can succeed in reading. Success is inherent in all activities in this chapter. The AD/HD student will be engaged, enriched, and empowered.

Mail Person on the Run

Students enjoy this activity because it enables, encourages, and empowers. A younger student who may be facing challenges in reading could really benefit from this activity. The parent gives the student a shoulder bag (not book bag) and then places index cards filled with messages into the bag. The student must read the card and act on these directions. Sometimes the parent might want to include spelling or vocabulary words on the cards. Each card is delivered and left at the relevant destination. Examples of messages could include:

- Go to your bedroom and get a book (card left in bedroom).

- Find the napkins and place them on the dinner table.

- See if the mail has arrived yet.

- Find the newspaper, and give it to me.

- Look out of the window and to see if there are any children outside.

- Check to see if there are any clothes in the dryer.

- What is the temperature in the house?

Students forget they are reading.

This activity empowers and engages.

Who Reads First?

It is not unusual for the AD/HD child to have difficulty reading and comprehending fiction and non-fiction. When parents and children read together, two goals are fulfilled: there is precious one-on-one time, and sharing the reading helps the student. The reading can be shared in many ways. Parent and child can read a different paragraph, a different page, or a different section. Since focusing is difficult, reading long segments can cause difficulty. So, when a parent finishes a section, the student must ask two or three questions to "make certain the parent understands" the material. Of course, when the student reads, the parent asks the questions. This often opens discussion and clarification.

This technique empowers the student while enabling him to succeed.

Read All About It

Printed material such as magazines, newspapers, advertisements, and junk mail can be useful educational materials. Activities should be age-appropriate. Depending upon the lesson for the day, the child can be asked to circle all the verbs, nouns, or adjectives. Other activities could be circling words with certain beginning or ending sounds, finding numbers, locating spelling words (if possible), blends, silent letters, letters that complete the alphabet, words that are new, and abbreviations. Then the circles can be connected with a pencil or crayon and some interesting shape might be outlined.

This is a calming activity that enables, enriches, and encourages success. Understanding that there will be a drawing project at the end is a motivator.

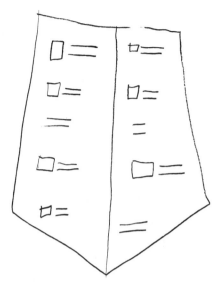

Follow the Line of Words

Many AD/HD students have difficulty tracking rows of words when reading. The method of holding a line marker under the row of words being read is common. However, at the end of the line of words being read, there is a break in the reading as the marker slides down to the next line. By holding the marker just above the line of words being read, and pushing it down when that line has been completed, the break is avoided. This allows for smooth reading and better comprehension.

The activity is enabling and empowering.

Family Pajama Party

Some people love to read. Some people hate to read. Some people do not have time to read. Some people will read only some things. Our fast-paced world does not allow time for everyone to read.

Plan a family pajama party for one night each week. Make popcorn and a healthy beverage. Perhaps order a pizza. When everyone in the family is prepared for bed, the whole family meets in one room, and everyone has a book in hand. Any appropriate reading material is permitted. Each family member finds a comfortable spot in the room (even under the table), and the next 40–60 minutes are devoted to silent reading time.

This activity is empowering, enabling, and engaging for the whole family.

Penlight Night

Bedtime is often a difficult time for children with AD/HD. Sometimes the child just cannot stop moving. Thoughts are racing and the idea of sleeping is not on the preferred list. Sometimes one of the side effects of medication is an inability to sleep. Nights can be very long.

Bedtime can become interesting. Allow the child to select a favorite book to take to bed. Then introduce a penlight (a very small handheld flashlight). Turn the lights out, and encourage reading with the penlight. Children love flashlights, the dark room is settling, and reading is encouraged. The penlight activity might be even more fun if the parent starts reading while the child holds the flashlight, but the parent should not stay too long. The activity should be time limited so that the child's eyes do not feel too strained. The child will calm down, relax, and enjoy the activity within this limited time span.

This activity empowers, enriches, and encourages.

Think About the Moral

The book *Aesop's Fables* can serve as an effective tool for the AD/HD student. Reading the fables and accompanying morals can address focus, executive functioning, and logical thinking. This book is most useful when shared with the parent. The reading can be shared, but the discussion of the moral should be led by the parent. Questions should help students to understand the relationship between the story and moral. Then the student can retell the story in a structured way, and apply the moral to the tale.

This activity enables and enriches.

Read, Rest, Relax

A comfortable sofa can become a great friend and enabler for the AD/HD child. When students must do assigned reading, fiction or non-fiction, sitting on a sofa next to an adult changes the nature of the task. While the adult is helping with the reading, sharing the questioning process, and discussing the material, the child is able to move away from the sterile learning environment and might relax enough to focus. Younger children may move closer and closer to the adult as the reading progresses.

The child is engaged, enriched, and enabled to enjoy the task.

5 Monster Math

Math is a subject dependent upon both memory and critical thinking. Most number problems rely on recall of basic facts, while word problems call for organization and processing information. These requirements can pose problems for the AD/HD student. One needs to focus to learn number facts, and one needs to manipulate information in word problems. As a result, math is double trouble for some students.

Some activities teach helpful little tricks for success in computing. Use of the highlighter (described in Chapter 3) can be helpful in math. The movement exercises in this chapter empower students by acknowledging their need to move. Some activities in this chapter are introduced as tricks, which are usually a source of fascination for children, allowing the child to become engaged.

Estimation

Almost all students have difficulty when asked to estimate things in the real world. Often it is difficult just distinguishing between feet and inches (or meters and centimeters), pounds and ounces (or kilograms and grams), or height and weight. You can start to "play" with estimation at any time. At home, it is wise to start estimating with hands-on activities. Before estimating anything, the child should be given a quick review of the reference point. For example, when using measurement estimation, show the child a yardstick (or meter stick) and point out inches and feet (or centimeters). This should not be a long lesson. The child's age determines how many parts of the category are introduced. Demonstrate and prove your answers using the yardstick (or meter stick). Then challenge the child to do more estimating within the category. Weight is easy to estimate using things in the kitchen.

This activity enables and enriches.

Math in Motion

Math is a subject that lends itself to addressing the challenges of focus and movement common to AD/HD students. The child can stand up during math and responses can be expressed in many ways. The answer to 5 – 3 can be jumped, or it can be answered with giant steps. The answer to the problem 6 + 7 can be clapped. An answer can be expressed with jumping jacks or toe touches. Large side-steps and backward steps are other ways to express answers.

The student is engaged, enabled, and enriched.

Silent Math

Silent math is a game that requires focus. No talking is allowed as math facts are practiced. The parent begins by holding up any number of fingers on one hand. The hand then draws an addition, subtraction, multiplication, or division sign in the air. Fingers on the other hand display the other half of the sum. The student uses fingers to display the answer. The problem is erased in air, and another problem is presented. The numbers are limited with only ten fingers to use, but students are engaged and math facts are practiced.

The child is empowered and encouraged.

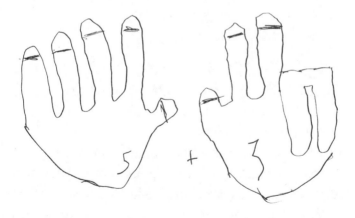

Math on a Grid

When students begin doing math processes such as two-digit multiplication and division, number placement becomes an issue. Determining how to align problems and how to manage multiples is difficult. The AD/HD student does not always have patience for this. So, using a word-processing program on the computer, make grids any size you wish. Begin with large squares. Once grids are made, the student needs to know one thing: *you never place more than one digit in a square.* When double-digit multiplication is introduced, remind the student that you multiply over the line and add under the line. This is often a confusing concept. Decisions about calculator use should be made based on the child's needs. The use of a calculator is discussed in the introduction.

The calculator and the graph enable and empower the student so encouragement is possible.

Long Division: A New Approach

Long division is a process that is very challenging. AD/HD students face an even greater challenge because division requires multiple processes, and multiple facts. The "DMSB" approach—Dad (divide), Mom (multiply), Sister (subtract), and Brother (bring down)—not only helps sequence the steps in division, but also engages students. The student must cross out the letter of each step as it is completed. Students must think, and their hands can be engaged while mastering the process.

Here is a guide to the approach:

1. 9	483 DMSB Dad, Mom, Sister, Brother	2. $\dfrac{5}{9\,|\,483}$ $48/9 = 5$ Divide $\longrightarrow$ Dad
3. $\dfrac{5}{9\,|\,483}$ $9 \times 5 = 45$ Multiply $\longrightarrow$ Mum	**4.** $\dfrac{5}{9\,|\,483}$ $\begin{array}{r} -45 \\ \hline 3 \end{array}$ $\begin{array}{r} 48 \\ -45 \\ \hline 3 \end{array}$ Subtract $\longrightarrow$ Sister
5. $\dfrac{5}{9\,|\,483}$ $45\downarrow$ 3 $\dfrac{5}{9\,|\,483}$ $45\downarrow$ 33 Bring down $\longrightarrow$ Brother	**6.** Start over at 33/9

The illustration uses a single-digit divisor for simplicity, but the same approach applies to multiple-digit divisors.

This activity is engaging.

Attacking the Word Problem in Math

Multi-step math word problems are a challenge to almost all children. They include information that needs sorting and organizing, which means that word problems are especially difficult for the AD/HD student. A parent should help with this process. Ideas for tackling the problems are listed below. Read the problem with the child. Discuss the problem by asking questions: What are they asking for? What information should we use? Are all the numbers important? Will the answer be stated in inches (or centimeters), spoons or animals? Once that process is complete, the child may require more coaching before trying to identify the mathematical operation/s required by the question. (See math clue words below.) Help her apply the proper mathematical symbols to the word problem. This activity engages her in the process, while empowering by achieving an understanding of the process.

- Read the problem twice and ask the student to define what the problem requires. Coaching might be necessary. Illustrations can be used to aid understanding.

- The student then reads the problem and tries to define the question. The parent may assist.

- The student uses a highlighter to point out the clue words (see below) and explains the importance of the highlighted words.

- All the numbers in the problem are written down and the child attempts to explain how to manipulate these numbers.

- The parent asks appropriate questions that will lead to solution of the problem.

Word problems require processing, organizing, and making associations. The AD/HD student will tire quickly and is apt to give up. These problems require parent patience, and the child should never be expected to complete more than two word problems a night. It is important to discuss this with the teacher.

This activity will enable and empower the student.

Math clue words

- Add/plus
- Altogether
- Average
- Calculator
- Check
- Divide/into
- Equal
- Estimate
- Greater than
- Highest
- How many
- In all
- Least
- Left
- Less than
- Lowest
- Mean
- Median

- Mode
- More
- Most

- Multiply/times
- Subtract

Checkbook Minder

If a parent chooses to use a token system to reward children, the stage is set for learning about checking accounts. A simplified deposit and withdrawal sheet can be generated to serve as a "checkbook." Children can use the checkbook to record token usage. The tokens themselves should be kept by the child at all times because they represent successes. This checkbook offers great practice for math facts, and helps children understand money management. The parent should monitor the first few transactions, and gradually allow the child to take over.

This activity empowers and enables.

Variations on Bingo

The traditional game of Bingo can be used in almost any subject. Because it is a game, it lends itself to instant success and encouragement. Each square on the card can hold an answer. In math, answers could be numbers or answers to basic fact questions; in social studies, answers could be words; in reading, words could be vocabulary. The card limits the number of choices so the student is not overwhelmed, and the game lends itself to a multi-sensory experience as he uses hands, eyes, and ears.

A "game" usually promotes a positive response, so the child is enabled and can be empowered when playing.

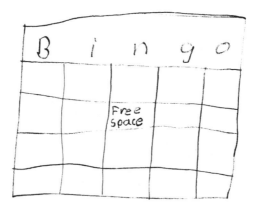

…ers in the correct place in a word. When …ng a new word, circle the silent letter so the …nows it is silent. Give her a worksheet with …ords containing silent letters to see if she can …he quiet ones. Help her make a list of common …mbinations and letters. Then see if she can fill …orrect silent letters in words on a worksheet. … silly, say the words by pronouncing the silent

… suggestions can empower and encourage.

…e Your Spelling Technique

…e AD/HD student is studying spelling words, …portant to try different techniques. Try not …se one method because variety will be more …. Some enabling techniques include: parent …dent writing a silly story using the words, …making a 'fill in the blank' story about the …aching the child how to use mnemonic devices, … words, singing words, or even taking a walk …rs to practice. Shoelaces or pipe cleaners can … to shape a word. The more senses involved in …, the more successful the child will be. …se activities enrich, encourage, and engage.

… and Pencil Spelling

…iditional paper and pencil approach in spelling … done creatively. The student can write silly …es using the words. The parent might be

6 Spelling

Spelling can be a daunting task for the child with AD/HD. Spelling requires memory, concentration, and the ability to manipulate words. Seeing a list of strange words each week and knowing the weekly expectations involved with the words add to inattention and restlessness. Activities in this chapter are designed to take the dread out of spelling for the AD/HD student. Each lesson is a motivator. If the student cannot handle the complete list of spelling words weekly, speak with the teacher about modifying the list.

Spell Three Ways

Learn to spell with color and texture. Children like to write with a variety of tools. Allow the child to write each spelling word three times, first with a gel pen, then a marker, and then a colored pencil. Next, permit her to write spelling words three times each with colored ink, crayon, and sparkle marker. Encourage the writing of each word three times in specific colors. For example, each word can be written three times in red or blue. These special implements should be used only for spelling. The different colors and textures become special spelling tools and may generate an interest in practicing spelling words. As children write the words with "fancy" implements, handwriting and coordination are practiced.

This activity engages and encourages.

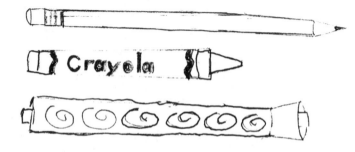

Technology as Success Enabler

The use of technology can be magic in spelling. Technology speaks to students of all ages, and is engaging, enabling, enriching, and empowering. Why not allow the child to text you the spelling words? You might then text the words to be learned back to him. Technology enables focus in many cases. Practice the spelling words by speaking to each other on the cell phone. Perhaps the spelling "test" could be emailed for correction.

These activities are engaging, enabling, and empowering.

Touch that Word

These techniques are chi… patience. The child's sei… techniques are great fun. … words with unusual substa… and time, shaving cream, s… paints can be used. The wo… be limited. For a more co… sand, cereal, beans, or brea… the word, the word shoul… pronounced loudly. The act… can be fun, and helps with…

This activity engages, e… child.

Just Plain Silent

There they are, those letters… and do not make a sound.… words the AD/HD student … there are few tricks to help w… There are, however, method…

silent le…
introduc…
student …
several v…
identify …
silent co…
in the c…
Just to b…
letters.
The…

Choo…
When t…
it is in…
to over…
enablin…
and st…
parent …
child, t…
jumpin…
outdoo…
be use…
learnir…
The…

Pape…
The t…
can b…
sente…

challenged to fill in the blanks of a student-generated sentence test. Another method to maintain interest might be a crossword puzzle. The puzzle can be created by the parent or student. The child uses the words either way. It might be fun writing clues and making the student a spelling detective. A letter scramble could be challenging and encourages the student to look up correct spellings. It is enjoyable writing words in the air. Allow the student to use his body to shape the word. This adds movement.

These activities empower and engage spellers.

7 Writing

Expressive writing is very difficult for the AD/HD student. Writing requires many processes. Getting ideas from head to paper while thinking about punctuation, neat writing, organization, and the urge to write down everything quickly can be overwhelming. On the other hand, the inability to focus, restlessness, and lack of ideas can plague a student. In this chapter, there are suggestions for making the writing experience more enjoyable. Each activity involves a writing task that is child-centered and incorporates a child-centered idea. These activities are enablers.

Attention, Babysitters

When empowered, the AD/HD student can produce amazing results. Asking the child to create something that would be useful for everyone in the family might be a motivating activity. It also enriches organizational skills and can be great focus practice. Ask the child to create a guide for babysitters in your home. Encourage brainstorming and then, if necessary, add some necessities to the list. This can be illustrated and written in a special book. Interesting creativity might emerge from this empowering activity. A guide for other things in the home also can be created—for example, a guide for dinner table manners or house rules.

This activity enables and encourages.

Hear and Draw

This is a break-time activity that stresses focusing and following directions. The adult gives verbal instruction while the student (and maybe a friend or sibling) attempts the exercise. There are two rules: the adult cannot repeat anything, and the children cannot talk to each other. The students draw what the adult says. For example, the parent may say: Draw one line down the middle of your paper. Then draw one line across the middle of your paper. Number the squares, one, two, three, four, beginning with the top left one. In number one, draw a circle…in number two write the alphabet, etc. The complexity of the instructions will depend upon the ages and capabilities of the student/s. Comparing pictures at the end is always fun.

This activity is engaging and empowering.

Recipe for Happiness

Child-created recipes can be very useful. These recipes are not used in the kitchen. Rather, they are recipes that can reveal some emotions the children experience. The parent decides whether the recipe must be written in complete sentences. The student can write recipes for a perfect day at home, a perfect day at school, perfect parents, how to be king of the world, or how to earn tokens. For example, a perfect day at home might consist of mixing one hour of extra sleep with a plate of breakfast in front of the television. Then add two friends for a play date followed by three choices for dinner. The day can be frosted with a three-mile trip to the ice cream store with Dad. It is important for the parent to review the recipes with the child.

The student is empowered and enabled.

No Homework? No Way!

"I don't have any homework today." *Wrong!* There is no such thing as a "no homework day" for a student with AD/HD. Remember that schedule, consistency, and routine are vital. There are many motivational and educational activities for such days. You might make a list of possible activities to give the student a choice. This empowers the child. Time the homework session as if it were a real homework day. Here are some activities you might consider:

- Read a high-interest book with your child.

- Learn math facts using the jump strategy method.

- The activity *What's for Dinner?* (page 87) is fun, especially when the student selects the categories.

- Read to the family pet.

- Write letters to friends and relatives.

- Plan a birthday party.

- Have fun with similes, metaphors, alliteration, and personification.

- Make a word search with the week's spelling words.

- Create an outline for a scrapbook to be made in the future.

- Make a crossword puzzle for the parents to do.

Any activity that engages, enables, and enriches the child is perfect. The games should be fun with an educational purpose.

Literary Elements

Introduce four popular literary elements so they are easily understood by the child.

- Simile: Comparing two things using the word "as" or "like."

- Metaphor: A comparison that does not use the words as or like.

- Alliteration: A group of words that begin with the same sound.

- Personification: Inanimate objects are given human characteristics.

The parent can determine how many of these terms the child is capable of handling. Select a theme such as big, happy, hungry, circus, school, cold, hot, etc. After doing some examples, give the child an opportunity to try using the elements. If sky is the theme, a simile might be "The sky is as blue as my eyes." A metaphor might be "The clouds are fluffy pillows." Alliteration might be "The silly sky sheds snow shoes secretly." Personification might describe clouds laughing at the sun. Use any or all of these elements, and encourage silly phrases.

This is an opportunity to giggle and play with the student.

Categorizing

Organization and focus are difficult skills for the AD/HD student. Placing things into proper categories is a way to practice organization. Practice can be fun and can be done in two ways. First, the child can be given the names of the categories as column headings and a list of words to place under the correct headings. Second, the student can be given a list of words and asked to work out what the categories are. At first, three categories will be enough. As the skill improves, more categories can be added.

This activity empowers and encourages.

Foam Ball Recall

A foam ball can be a child's best study buddy. It can be used in any subject area. It addresses focusing.

The parent asks a question and throws the ball to the student. The student returns the ball with the correct response (hints are allowed). This engages the child in a movement game that focuses on test preparation.

This is an enabling and encouraging activity.

Searching for Details

This versatile activity addresses focus. It is helpful for every parent to have something like this in the survival kit. The activity can be used for a rest time or short homework break. Find a picture in a book, magazine, newspaper, or even online. The selected picture should be very detailed. The artist Pieter Brueghel painted many detailed pictures of children and games. As you look at the picture with your child, see if the child can locate something in the picture following your directions, clues, or hints. Try to focus on a small detail. Spot-the-difference puzzles also address focusing. These are one-on-one activities which makes them special. They should not take up a lot of time.

This activity is engaging, empowering, and encouraging.

Who, What, Where, When, Why

The five Ws (who, what, where, when, and why) can be used to help the AD/HD student structure writing pieces. The student could write a paragraph including the Ws, or the Ws could be stressed in an oral presentation.

The Ws are helpful to the student when they are used to practice categorization and organization.

There are several ways to use the five Ws. Make five columns and head each with one of the W words. Challenge the student to place words or phrases in each column. The child can then be asked to write a sentence using words from some or all columns. In another activity the parent can call out one word at a time, and the child can identify the category.

These games engage and enrich children.

What's for Dinner?

Expressive writing is a scary prospect for many children. Putting thoughts down on paper in a logical order and with correct punctuation is a difficult task for the

AD/HD student. An interesting method to initiate the process begins by asking the child to think of a favorite food. The choice is a secret. The adult also thinks of a favorite food. Parent and child both write five sentences about their respective choices, *without* naming the food. Just describe the food. The first sentence should be a topic sentence, such as "Many people love my favorite food because…" The descriptions are read aloud, and each person attempts to guess the other's favorite. This activity engages the child and enriches the writing process. When guessing is done, you might encourage the student to think of another category to use for description. All comments about the writing should be positive.

This game encourages the child to continue writing and enables written expression.

Restaurant Review

As a reward for some accomplishment, the child might be permitted to select a restaurant for a family dinner. Beforehand, a professional restaurant review could be discussed. These reviews are found in newspapers, magazines, and online. Read and discuss the review with the student. Make sure to discuss all the things that are considered in a restaurant review: atmosphere, presentation, decor, noise level, and service. The child can make observations during dinner in order to write a review of the chosen restaurant. This activity encourages writing and judgment. It is fun to send the review to the restaurant. Quite often there is a surprise response from the restaurant.

This activity is empowering for the child.

The Envelope, Please

An interesting way to make the writing process painless begins with an envelope. Both parent and student can suggest three writing topics. The adult suggestions should be child-oriented. Each suggestion will be written on a separate piece of paper and placed in the envelope. The student selects a topic from the envelope. Between three and five sentences (age-appropriate) can be written about the topic.

This enables the student to participate in the selection and encourages expressive writing.

Wanted

Motivating activities create an interest in descriptive writing. Ask the student to make a wanted poster. The poster can include a picture, and the subject of the hunt can be selected by the child. This activity allows the child to use descriptive words and to decide who is wanted and why. Description should be in complete sentences, and should include a reason for wanting the particular subject. Prompts could include hair color, eye color, height, weight, habits, and personality.

This activity empowers and engages.

Invitations

When children invite friends to parties or sleepovers, invitations are appropriate. Some invitations are computer-generated, some are done by hand, and some are purchased. In any case, it is important for the student to know what information must go on an invitation, and the information must be communicated in a timely fashion. The information must include who, what, where, when, purpose of party, and necessary instructions (bring a towel or a sleeping bag). RSVP details with a phone number should be included. Invitations should not be delivered in school, but should be mailed or delivered to invitees' homes. It is always nice to include some original artwork from the sender. As a pretend exercise, you could encourage the child to make an invitation to a sleepover for a favorite movie star, TV character, or stuffed animal. When the invitation is complete, the parent should verify that all information is included.

This exercise is empowering, enriching, and encouraging.

A Fairy Tale

Making up and writing fairy tales offers a unique experience. They have some structure and allow the child to walk in a land that is self-created. The characters are fashioned by the student. Fairy tales always begin with "Once upon a time." Everything happens in threes (three bears, three billy goats, three pigs). Fairy tales sometimes end with "They all lived happily after." The story can be written, done with puppets, acted out, or told.

This activity empowers, engages, and enriches.

Thank You Notes

Thank you notes should be handwritten. The AD/HD student may be capable of only one sentence on each note. If that is the case, the child needs to know that it is important to thank a person for something specific. "Thank you" or "Thank you for the gift" is not enough. If more than one sentence is possible, it is advisable to say how or when the gift will be used. The child's own artwork can be included. A thank you note is never a negative document. Ask your child to write a thank you note on behalf of a family pet or on behalf of some inanimate object in the home.

Writing a proper thank you note is a social skill that empowers and engages.

The Employment Application

Writing does not always have to be in composition form. This activity has a three-part focus: writing, organization, and thoughtful questioning. The student will create an employment application. The application will be for the job of school teacher. Before the application is created, discuss the need for basic information, educational experiences, "what if" questions, and those hard questions that require thought, such as ideas about how to handle situations, students, and school rules. It is important to ask why the applicant would like the job. Encourage the child to organize the questions in different sections. When she has finished creating the application, a parent should review it, and may need to remind her about some questions.

This is an empowering and encouraging activity.

Interview the Principal

This activity serves two purposes. First, it relates to social skills and, second, it helps the child ask questions, and then organize and present replies in a structured fashion. The child will be interviewing the principal of the school so all students will learn about the head of the school. First, a list of questions must be generated. The parent can help with this list. The interview can focus on the principal's education, family, job details, and philosophy of education. The student is responsible for making an appointment and conducting an interview. Students should be taking notes during the interview. When the interview is complete, notes can be organized into the above-mentioned categories, and an article for the school newspaper can be written.

This activity empowers, engages, and enriches.

Parts of Speech

Learning the parts of speech and labeling them is an activity that most children dislike intensely. Learning rules might be especially difficult for the AD/HD child who has difficulty focusing or sitting still. Using a plastic table cloth or a large roll of paper, trace round the child who lies on top of the paper. You might want to do this with poster board and draw the shape of the person on it. Use three different colored writing implements and make a key at the bottom of the paper. For example, red is for nouns, blue is for verbs, and green is for adjectives. With the red marker, ask the student to label some parts of the body with nouns: hand, foot, head, eye. With the blue marker, he labels the same body parts with words that tell what the body part does: hand touches, eye sees, foot walks, head thinks. With the green marker, ask him to add a describing word to the chosen body parts: big hands, bony knees.

This activity promotes movement, helps the student learn the parts of speech, enables him to be successful, and requires complete engagement.

Words for Pictures

The hesitant writer can be empowered by using pictures. Pictures can be generated from any source: newspapers, books, internet, magazines, and comic books. "Happy" pictures are preferable for these activities. The pictures can be used to write captions, titles, dialogue, stories, and poems. Some pictures might require sentences, phrases, or just one word. The language practice should address the child's specific needs.

A good way to engage a student in a longer writing process is through the use of comic strips. Present a comic strip that does not have words. The child can fill in the bubbles. The student quickly becomes engaged in creating the story.

This activity is empowering.

8 Addressing Symptoms

This chapter presents activities and suggestions to address some specific symptoms of AD/HD. It includes recommendations for the study area, methods to deal with impulsivity, taking care of the wiggles, planning, and practice with directions. Several of the activities can be personalized by using examples from the child's life. There are activities that conclude with a discussion. These activities encourage and enrich, and may also engage the student.

Impulsivity

The impulsivity that accompanies AD/HD can be very difficult to control. The child may act without thinking and express frustration in any setting. Impulsivity includes hitting, throwing, running, screaming, and refusing to do things. This behavior can alienate the child from friends, family, and teachers. Although difficult, the adult should avoid negativity. This activity helps the student to think and talk about the impulsivity. A stack of prepared cards is used for this activity. A decision-making situation is written on each card. The student selects a card and must come up with three responses to the situation. Then the best of the three responses is chosen and explained. This activity enables the child to understand that there are multiple ways to solve a problem. Some situations requiring a decision are suggested below.

This activity empowers.

Making choices

- Cinderella's stepmother makes her do all the chores. Cinderella goes to speak to her.

- The tortoise beats the hare in the race. The hare goes to speak to the tortoise afterwards.

- Dorothy is under attack from the Wicked Witch of the West. Dorothy needs to come up with a plan to deal with her enemy.

- Your teacher has forgotten recess time.

- You left your math book in school and need to tell your parents.

- Your sibling slips and falls.

- Another student hits you.

- Your parents take your cell phone as a punishment.

- Your sibling tells on you.

- Someone takes your pencil without permission.

- Your friend kicks you.

- People are throwing popcorn during a movie.

- You do not like the food your parents cooked for dinner.

- You are put in time out.

- You want to say something important and adults are talking.

- Your friend will not let you on the baseball team.

- You miss the deadline for soccer sign-up.

- Kids in your class laugh at you when you ask a question.

- Your parents will not let you go to sports practice because your homework is not done.

- A kid in school pushes you really hard.

- Your dog ate your favorite shoes.

- You are involved in a big fight at school that you did not start.

- The teacher lost your homework.

- You forgot to study for a test.

Impulse Patrol

Impulsivity is a symptom of AD/HD. This symptom is a cause for concern both at home and at school. A student needs to know and understand expectations. Then, when there is a problem, the expectation can be discussed. Both at home and in school, it is important not to call negative attention to the impulsive behavior. The tendency is to punish, but punishment does not address the behavior. At home, if danger is not a consideration, let the behavior play out, and then alternative forms of behavior can be discussed. During the discussion, include three important questions: What did you do? Why did you do it? What are three alternatives you could use next time? Permitting the child to analyze her behavior empowers her to alter the behavior in the future.

Happy Birthday

Planning, organizing, and anticipating consequences are very difficult tasks for the AD/HD student. This activity empowers the student to practice these skills. Tell the student that there will be a birthday party in the home. Offer the basic details: time, place, number of guests, includes lunch, movie after lunch. Ask the child to make a list of everything that must be done and purchased for the party. First, make a grocery list, then think about decorations. Detail preparations on another page, and make a list of all preparations in the order they must be done. Allow as much time as needed. If handwriting is a problem, the computer can be used.

When the list is complete, discuss it with the child. Discussions about sequencing can result.

This activity engages, encourages, and enables.

No Noise Allowed

The AD/HD student is sensitive to any distraction such as a dog barking, the sound of an ice cube in a glass, a ringing phone, or even a paper flapping in the wind. Distractions become the focus of the AD/HD student's attention. To help block out auditory distractions, it is helpful to have a set of earphones in the study area.

Allow the student to decorate the earphones, name them, and make them a welcome part of the learning experience. The child can simply name their headphones something like "John's headphones," or can give them fun names like "Silent Ears" or "The Quiet Headband."

The earphones enrich the learning experience and encourage focusing.

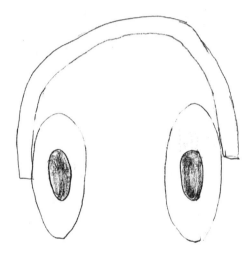

Stretch and Pull

A rubber band ball can be very useful in the study area. It can be held, squeezed, pulled, and dismantled. A fidgeting problem is addressed when the ball is held and squeezed. Frustration is addressed by pulling and dismantling the ball. Rubber bands can be added or removed during thinking time. The student could be challenged to start a new ball or could demolish an existing ball. Anxiety is addressed using the ball.

This activity is engaging and encourages the child to release tensions in an appropriate fashion.

Bursting Bubbles

A box or bag filled with bubble wrap can be very useful when working with an AD/HD child. The supply of wrap should be readily accessible at all times. When the student's frustration becomes intense, a trip to the bubble wrap area is a good idea. It is fun to pop the bubbles, requires some strength, and is great for tension release. This enables the child to release tension appropriately.

Getting to Know You

Appropriate social skills pose a problem for many AD/HD students. Because of many AD/HD behaviors, peers are seldom keen to bond with the child. It is necessary to practice methods of communication. When you wish to get to know someone, you ask questions hoping to find common ground. The student is on the floor ready for sit-ups. (If sit-ups are too difficult, he can do stand-up/sit-downs.) Challenge the child to create questions that would help to learn about a new friend. Each time the child asks an appropriate, relevant question, three sit-ups are required. This activity will foster communication skills. The parent records the questions so that they may later be used for role playing.

This activity builds an awareness of other people, while engaging, enriching, and encouraging.

Exercise Your Memory

There are several activities that exercise the student's memory and can be done anytime or anywhere. Place several objects on a tray. For example, use a spoon, napkin, book, pencil, apple, key, phone, and other things from around the house. Allow the student to look at the tray for 60 seconds. Take the tray away and remove one item from it. Show it to the child again. See if she can name the missing object. Another activity with the tray involves asking the student to remember all things on the tray when you remove it.

These activities enable, empower, and encourage.

Focus and Concentration

An old-fashioned game called "Drop the Clothespin in the Bottle" is a great way to address concentration and focus difficulties in AD/HD children. All that is needed is one clothespin (clothes peg) and one bottle. The clothespin is held at waist level, and the bottle is on the ground. The child stands over the bottle, and attempts to drop the clothespin in it. If this is too difficult and too frustrating for him, try using a wide-mouthed jar to increase the possibility of success. He must concentrate to master the necessary technique. This is a slow-moving activity, but the challenge and possibility of success is great.

This game is engaging and empowering.

Playmates

This activity is intended to help the student understand the importance of socializing. Being an AD/HD student can be very isolating. Behavior and inappropriate actions can alienate the child. Using paper or a white board divided into three columns labeled "One," "Two," and "More," assist the student in naming recreational activities. Baseball goes in the third column, because it requires many people for a game. Tennis goes in the second column. Most computer games will go in the first column. Do not lecture, and do not imply that the child is a loner. Help her to draw some gentle conclusions after the activity.

This activity addresses social skills, and empowers and encourages students.

Fidget Away

An inability to focus, especially in school, often results in inappropriate behaviors. These are the trips to the drinking fountain, tapping on a desk, squirming in the chair, and often disrupting other students. If the AD/HD student is engaged, classroom interruptions may decrease. With the teacher's approval, children with AD/HD might benefit from a fidget box in the desk. A small box or pencil case can be filled with objects that can be manipulated quietly when the urge to move arises. The contents might include pipe cleaners, squish balls, cotton balls, rubber animals, erasers, and play dough. The fidget box is a distraction that may temper inappropriate behaviors because the child will be occupied.

This activity is engaging and encouraging.

Twenty Questions

Many assignments require full-sentence responses. This means that the response begins with the words in the question. An AD/HD student might have difficulty with this process because two steps are involved: writing a complete sentence, and thinking about an answer. The student can begin by thinking of a relative or friend. The parent is allowed 20 information-seeking questions to identify the person. However, each answer must begin with the words in the question. For example, the parent might ask, "Why did you select your secret character?" The response could be "I selected my secret character because I like the way he talks." Of course, parent and child can change roles. It is helpful if the questions require responses of more than one word. Question starters that might require multiple word answers include: tell me about, how do you describe, if…then, why, and explain.

This activity encourages, enables, engages, and enriches.

For Sale

Selling something requires organization, focus, and some social skills. It also requires the ability to make the item for sale attractive to the buyer. Most AD/HD students have difficulty with these skills, but can practice using them by trying to sell something. Ask the child to get a favorite toy to be "sold," but assure the child that this is a game. Help the child look in some magazines or newspapers to find powerful words that could be used to sell something. This can be an oral or written activity. In order to make the sale, the following areas must be addressed: the reason for sale, an excellent description, and how the price was decided. Perhaps the student could create a colorful poster to help the sale. This should be an independent activity for the student. After the sales pitch, offer to buy the toy, and praise the student's efforts all you can. Then discuss what made the sales pitch so good.

This activity stresses empowerment and enrichment.

Why are There Rules?

This is a game the whole family might enjoy. It is particularly important for the AD/HD student because it stresses the importance of rules and organization. Find a game that is new to everyone in the family. Often the dollar store has unfamiliar card games; board games will work, too. Encourage the family to gather around a table to play the game. Beforehand, remove *all* instructions from the game. When everyone is ready to play, confusion and discussion result because nobody will know what to do. People will react in different ways. Some will create a game, some will walk away, some will sulk. The confusion will end after a few minutes when the instructions may appear. The discussion that follows should illustrate how difficult it is to function without rules. The rules allow everybody to have fun.

This is an empowering activity.

9 Emotions

The AD/HD child can have very strong feelings that often remain unexpressed or are expressed inappropriately. Emotions are exhibited through temper tantrums, impulsive behavior, crying, or angry outbursts. Introducing the child to a variety of methods to communicate emotions might help to neutralize the behavior. This chapter includes creative dramatics, coloring, "reading" faces, and the opportunity to discuss feelings. These activities might be used during the homework time as frustrations build, or they can be encouraged at any other time.

These activities encourage and enrich, and might allow emotions to be exhibited appropriately in the future.

How Do You Feel?

When AD/HD students come home from a long day at school, they arrive hungry, tired, and filled with thoughts. They could have been subjected to teasing and teacher criticism, and felt confusion and anger in school. On the other hand, they could feel successful, happy, and full of pride. Sometimes the child is unwilling to share emotions. After the half-hour down time with a snack, it is helpful to initiate a conversation. This can be done by asking four questions:

- How are you?

- What is the best thing that happened in school today?

- What is the worst thing that happened in school today?

- Is there anything you would like to discuss with me?

If silence is the child's preference, honor that decision, and start the homework process. If there is a problem, it probably will be shared with you during one-on-one time. It is important for the child to release any angry emotions.

This activity enables and encourages.

Color Me Happy

An interesting way to allow the AD/HD student to express those deep-down emotions is to draw pictures. When the drawing is for an invisible audience, it is often easier to express feelings. Ask the child to make a coloring book for a young sibling, friend, or neighbor to color, illustrating a different emotion on each page.

There can be a sentence under each picture. When it is completed, offer to deliver the book for another child to color.

This is engaging, empowering, and enabling. The presentation of feelings will be interesting.

Helping Hands

The AD/HD student, like most children, loves to please parents and teachers. One way to help him please his parent is to ask him to do something that helps the adult. The responsibility needs to be desirable (not retrieving garbage cans), and should be fashioned as a success experience for the student. At home, he could be responsible for walking the dog, watering plants, feeding the pets, bringing in the mail, unloading the dishwasher, or helping serve dinner. Success and compliments should be given generously. It is best to change the responsibility weekly so the job does not become boring and task-like.

This activity encourages and empowers.

Creative Dramatics

Creative dramatics is a great outlet for the AD/HD child. It allows students to be someone or something different, and encourages self-expression and interpretation. The parent can request that the child become a certain person, place, or thing. For example, she might be asked to be the Tin Man, or a doctor, or a school teacher. Or she could pretend to be a chair or can opener. If there is a willing sibling available, the two children can work together to create a fork or bathtub. This activity can be done with or without words.

This activity empowers and engages, and is a success experience.

Read My Face

Homework time can be accompanied by a lot of grumbling and whining. It can also include frustration, tension, anger, and the feeling of inadequacy. Often children do not know how to express feelings in appropriate, meaningful ways. This activity may help the AD/HD child to express those strong feelings. Use the pictures of faces below. Ask which picture best defines how the child is feeling. This activity can be done in three parts. First, the parent points to a face and asks, "What is that person saying?" The second time the faces are used, tell the student to pretend that the face belongs to a teacher. "What is this teacher saying?" Next, the student can pretend that the faces are self-portraits. "What would you be saying?" Of course, the faces can represent any number of people. This activity can be used as a minor break when tension is high.

The student is empowered and encouraged to express emotions.

Family Meeting

The behavior of a child with AD/HD can have an effect on the entire family. Siblings often feel ignored. Adults are exhausted from controlling their anger and frustration. The child cannot control his behavior. Tension builds, and quality family time seems to slip away. It is very important for the family to address these feelings.

When the child is calm, it is appropriate to have a family meeting. These meetings should occur consistently and frequently. Blame and anger are forbidden during these meetings. Punishment is also forbidden. The purpose of the family meeting is to express feelings so that everyone understands how one person's behavior affects everyone else. All statements should begin with "I feel," and it is vital that the AD/HD child does not become the major subject. Both positive and negative feelings should be expressed. The goal is not resolution but to understand that, in a family, everyone is affected by everyone else.

This meeting should result in self-reflection. This empowers, enables, and encourages everyone in the home.

Talking Silently

People communicate in many ways. Non-verbal communication is challenging. In this activity, the parent asks a question and the student replies non-verbally. This activity is similar to charades minus all the rules. It is also another way to learn about emotions. At homework time it might be interesting to allow the student to charade responses to some academic questions. This is a form of creative dramatics. The parent could pose these questions:

- What is your favorite subject?

- How was your day in school today?

- How do you feel when you win a token?

- Who is your best friend?

- What is your favorite sport?
- How do you feel when you do homework?
- What is the best family activity?
- What is your favorite food?
- What makes a person happy?

This activity is engaging and encouraging.

Teamwork

Empowering the AD/HD student, while encouraging some teamwork in the family, can have rewards for all. This technique can be used with academics or behavior modification. Allow the AD/HD student to be responsible for an enjoyable family "happening." For example, if she can finish all morning chores this week without complaining, the family can have a game night. Or, if she can remember to complete her school planner for three days this week, the family can go out for dinner on the weekend. The reward should be attractive to the whole family in order to motivate them to use teamwork to assist in achieving the goal. The team can encourage the child to fulfill the requirements.

The activity empowers the student while promoting family unity.

Demonstrate the Sport

Involvement in a sport is recommended for the AD/HD student. Although the practices and games can encroach on homework time, the opportunity to move and be involved with others and the possible opportunity for a success experience often outweigh the loss of study time. The willingness to partake in a sport varies with each child. It is important for each child to be aware of the available opportunities. A movement game with input from parent and child can help with this. The student will mime a key action for different sports, while the parent guesses the sport. When the student runs out of ideas, the parent can suggest other sports to demonstrate. Another way to do this involves the parent making all the suggestions, while the student mimes the moves.

This game creates awareness, but, of course, is not a guarantee that the student will join a team. Empowerment, enrichment, and engagement are key purposes of this activity.

Vegetable Shows

Another type of creative dramatics for home or school is a puppet show. In this activity, vegetables are used as characters. Regular puppets usually have some human features. When vegetables are used, the lack of human characteristics frees the operator even more. Wonderful shows can be presented using carrots, celery, cucumbers, broccoli "trees," and any color peppers. Any vegetable can be used. The student animates these characters, and can express some strong feelings in the plays written, produced, and performed by the child. It is important to put a time limit on the show because it can get quite long.

This activity empowers, enriches, and encourages students.

Thinking Ahead

Thinking into the future is a very difficult skill for AD/HD students. Not only is it difficult to think about consequences of behavior, but AD/HD students have problems thinking about making and achieving goals. The student would benefit from some practice making short-term goals. Discuss goals and their importance. Help the child create a goal that can be fulfilled by dinner time that day. Ensure that the goals are easily achievable. Examples of short-term goals could be: will not complain about homework, will do a daily chore without being reminded, or will remember the planner. The child can be rewarded if the goal is fulfilled. One success will lead to another. Longer-term goals can be added gradually. Slowly, move away from life goals and make academic goals.

This activity empowers, enriches, and encourages.

Time Capsule

This activity involves looking to the future. AD/HD students have difficulty with the concept of time. It is important that the student is given a realistic and familiar frame of reference. References might include: when you are my age, when you are a parent, when you go to high school, or when you are Grandma's age. Talk with the child about change. There were no computers years ago; cell phones, computer games, Wii, and iPad did not exist. The child should begin thinking about the future. Ask him to think about what people in the future might wish to know about today. He should think of five items that will tell people in the future about today, and place these things (or representations of them) in a metal box to preserve them for the future. Help him put the metal box in the garage or ground.

This activity empowers and enriches.

Confronting the Wiggles

These are suggestions for movement activities to use for a short amount of time when you get the signals that the child just can't sit still anymore.

- Jumping jacks
- Hop on one foot
- Hop like a rabbit
- Touch your toes ten times
- Clap your hands over your head
- Skip
- Jump
- Kick your legs in front, to the back, and to the sides
- Jump like a frog
- Rock back and forth
- Turn three times
- Sit, stand three times
- Pretend you are hula-hooping
- Pat your head while rubbing your tummy
- Stoop down and stand up three times
- Three sit-ups

Conclusion

Parents for Progress

This activity book does not offer any cures. It is intended to help students and parents handle the difficult homework time each day. The combination of anxious adults and tired, resistant students is not conducive to progress. The activities in the book engage, enable, encourage, enrich, and empower AD/HD students. They are geared to keep this time tension free. It might even evolve into fun time. The parent must think about planning, praising, persevering, prioritizing, and remaining positive.

Because homework time is often parent-dependent, it is important to *plan* ahead daily. Dinner should be made, siblings should be engaged in other parts of the home, phone calls should be avoided, and the parent needs to focus on progress. It is also helpful to have supplies close at hand, especially on days when the *Scavenger Hunt* (page 23) is not used.

Many teachers now place weekly homework assignments online. Keeping in mind that it is the student's responsibility to keep track of homework, the parent can use these online reminders to monitor homework. Additionally, teachers are sometimes willing to alert the parent about future progress expectations. For those parents who can retrieve homework assignments online, it is helpful to consider how best to motivate the child using some of the activities in this book.

Praise is the most important tool a parent can use. It should be consistent, immediate, and honest. Certainly, praise should be bestowed on any academic accomplishment. If you cannot praise academics at first, then praise anything that contributes to homework success (neat backpack, remembering lunch box, having planner at home, handwriting, paying attention, attitude, etc.). Praise is a motivator.

The parent must *persevere*. Allow the student to be incorrect. Overlook some mistakes. Respect the strategies the student develops. The assignment might not have the appearance you desire, but the student owns it. Engage everything in your power to remain calm and accepting. It isn't easy, but anger and disagreement don't finish homework. An upset child never finishes homework. Insults, put downs, and impatience are counterproductive. If the parent needs to take a walk to control frustration, it is OK. Often, a student's mood and enthusiasm reflect the parent's attitude. The parent's mood often dictates the mood of the day.

Setting *priorities* is central to any homework session. Sometimes, there is just too much homework, and you must decide what to save for the next day. Sometimes the student is just having a plain horrible day. Do you insist on homework, or partial homework, or break? Do you notify the teacher about there being too much homework? Which subject is most important for the child? How much is enough? Do you request more time for assignments? Is a homework dose of medication required? You can make any decisions based upon the best interest of your child. Priorities might not be the same each day.

Put your energies into making the homework session fun. Make it a *positive* experience. The side effect of removing the pressure enriches the homework time. It also allows for some ver y valuable parent/child time. It is a great way to bond. Why not make it positive?

I understand that all activities in the book require constant supervision by the parent. I understand also that often there are siblings in the home, the parent has worked for an entire day, dinner must be served, mail must be opened, and phone calls need returning. My hope is that the creation of a positive environment will become the usual, and parent supervision can be reduced slowly. When you and the student are ready, experiment! Leave the scene for five minutes. Increase and decrease time away based on student progress.

Index